How to Conduct
Collaborative Action
Research

RICHARD SAGOR

 Association for Supervision and Curriculum Development Alexandria, Virginia USA

Association for Supervision and Curriculum Development
1703 N. Beauregard St. • Alexandria, VA 22311-1714 USA
Telephone: 1-800-933-2723 or 703-578-9600 • Fax: 703-575-5400
Web site: http://www.ascd.org • E-mail: member@ascd.org
Author guidelines www.ascd.org/write

ASCD publications present a variety of viewpoints. The views
expressed or implied in this publication should not be interpreted
as official positions of the Association.

Printed in the United States of America.

ISBN-13: 978-0-87120-201-7
ASCD Stock No.: 61193011

Library of Congress Cataloging-in-Publication Data

Sagor, Richard
How to conduct collaborative action research / Richard Sagor.
    p.   cm.
Includes bibliographical references.
ISBN 0-87120-201-8 : $6.95
    1. Action research in education—United States—Methodology.
I. Title.
LB1028.25.U6S24   1993
370′.78′073—dc20   92-40296
                                                                   CIP

10 09 08 07   15   14   13   12   11

How to Conduct Collaborative Action Research

Preface

DURING THE PAST THREE YEARS, MY COLLEAGUES AND I HAVE HAD THE privilege of working with hundreds of teachers from dozens of schools in a loosely knit consortium called Project LEARN (League of Educational Action Researchers in the Northwest). With support and training from the developers of Project LEARN, teams of teachers in the participating schools went through a process designed to help them use collaborative action research to improve teaching and learning conditions in their schools and classrooms. Many of the ideas in this book are part of the Project LEARN training model, and many of the examples given come from teachers who have been part of the consortium. Keep in mind, however, that action research is a dynamic field in which no two people share precisely the same perspective. Don't be surprised if some of the ideas and definitions shared here differ a bit from what you may have read elsewhere about action research.

As you read through this book, you will notice that I often use the voice of the first person plural: we. I used this pronoun because in writing this book, I felt constantly in the company of all the teachers I have ever worked with.

I am particularly indebted to my colleague Peter Holly. Peter was the original Project LEARN trainer, and it was his conception of the action research process that informed our training programs and, consequently, the process elaborated on in this book.

I also wish to thank all the teachers in Project LEARN for allowing me to learn with you as you reflected on your teaching and on the learning of your students.

Finally, special thanks go to Dea Cox, perhaps the world's greatest reflective practitioner, and the staff at the West Linn (Oreg.) School District, who are living proof that when schools are built around people and when professional talent is respected, nurtured, and rewarded, schools become extraordinary places where children thrive.

—RICHARD SAGOR

1
Why We Need Collaborative Action Research

ON SOME ISSUES OF SCHOOLING, THERE SEEMS TO BE NO DISPUTE. No one would question that fostering student growth and development is the primary objective of our public school system. Likewise, no thoughtful observer would disagree that student growth and development are the direct result of instructional interactions between student and teacher. When we hold these twin beliefs—that schools are about student learning and that learning occurs primarily through the efforts and talents of teachers—then it becomes clear that school reform should focus on nurturing and developing the teaching profession. The highest priority of school reform should be to create conditions that support teachers in their work and make teaching an attractive option for the best and brightest college graduates.

Unfortunately, many of the more celebrated restructuring initiatives focus on issues regarding school governance, financing, the use of technology, and innovative instructional strategies. Although all these efforts have some potential for improving the teaching environment (and, consequently, the learning environment), I believe they skirt the central issue, which is restructuring the teaching profession itself. But why, you may ask, is restructuring necessary? And how does collaborative action research fit in? To answer the first question, let's contrast teaching with several other professions and examine some areas where it falls short.

Teaching Versus Other Professions

A few key factors clearly distinguish public school teaching from other service professions. Understanding these factors will make it easier to see why teaching is not often viewed as an attractive option by bright college graduates.

Isolation from Other Professionals

Follow a doctor, a lawyer, an engineer, or an architect for a day, and it becomes obvious that they spend as much time interacting with their colleagues as they do serving their clients. A doctor discusses the meaning of an X-ray with other physicians and healthcare workers, a lawyer consults with associates on trial strategy, and engineers and architects work in teams to develop new prototypes and designs. Interactions with other professionals stimulate and push these people to new levels of performance in both the art and the craft of their profession.

Teachers work in a different world. Roland Barth likened American teachers to a group of preschoolers engaged in parallel play. Although they may work in a building with other teachers and even use the same materials and follow the same schedule, they rarely turn to one another during the school day except during their thirty-minute lunch period, where informal norms often forbid any kind of professional talk. This dearth of collegial stimulation would be bad enough if teaching were a profession with a certain and finite knowledge base. But the problems of teaching are ever changing, and absolute solutions are usually not to be found. Successful teaching is a mixture of art and craft honed through experience. In such a profession, a lack of meaningful discourse with fellow professionals can have disastrous effects.

In surveys of promising young teachers who decided to abandon education after only a few years in the classroom, professional isolation has been one of the most frequently cited dissatisfiers. If we continue to expect teachers to solve increasingly complex educational problems by themselves, we can forget about widespread excellence in the classroom. Most inquisitive and collaborative people will continue to shy away from teaching. And those who do take the plunge will probably confine themselves to the few teaching strategies they've found are easiest for them to use, keeping their door shut for fear of exposing to colleagues that they have not yet mastered this unmasterable craft.

Contributions to the Knowledge Base

All professions are informed by a knowledge base, and teaching is no exception. We have a body of accepted research literature on effective teaching practices and successful schooling techniques. As in other professions, teachers are expected to be familiar with, make use of, and respect the foundations of their practice. But in all the professions *except* teaching, practitioners are also expected to interact with and contribute to the development of their profession's knowledge base.

For instance, pick up any medical journal and you will find that most of the articles are written by practicing physicians. The formats are remarkably similar. The author first explains the patient's symptoms and then details the treatment. The author/physician concludes by sharing the results of the treatment. The function of this medical literature is to alert other physicians to what colleagues are learning. Were I a doctor reading such articles, I would ask myself: (1) Do my patients have similar symptoms? and (2) If they do, should I attempt similar interventions?

The story for other professions runs along the same lines. Engineers work from a knowledge base created by generations of engineers and learn continually from their colleagues; their work, in turn, informs the next generation of innovation. Architects draw plans based on the work of other architects, and lawyers construct briefs and legal arguments based on the experience of other lawyers.

Once again, teachers are different. Most educational journals (with the notable exception of *Educational Leadership*) do not feature the work of public school teachers. Instead, they are vehicles for the dissemination of ideas, commentaries, and studies from professors, consultants, administrators, and the like, who work outside the world of the classroom. The topics, problems, or issues pursued are significant, but not necessarily helpful to teachers on the front line. The context of the interventions reported or discussed in the education journals comprising our knowledge base may or may not conform to the realities of the public school classroom. In education, the worlds of research and practice are both separate and unequal, for the teacher who ignores research is likely seen as anti-intellectual or unprofessional, whereas the researcher who ignores the classroom bears no such label.

In fact, policymakers and supervisors often demand that teachers implement this externally derived educational research in their classrooms. The prevailing paradigm in education is one of the supervisor telling workers how to do their work because the supervisor supposedly has superior knowledge. This model is not without precedent. It is the very model of blue-collar work: The foreman always knows best, and it is the line workers' job to simply follow directions and meet his expectations. While that approach is increasingly seen as problematic in the trades, it is clearly disastrous for endeavors that we think of as professional. Until teachers become involved in generating the knowledge that informs their practice, they will remain cast as subordinate workers rather than dynamic professionals.

Separation of Quality Control

In most professions, standards of excellence emerge from the profession itself. The work of the master establishes the target for others who follow. Furthermore, monitoring the bottom line is seen as necessary for maintaining a professional edge. Self-monitoring helps professionals set their own improvement agendas. For example, by examining the needs of their patients and the results of their work, doctors determine where their professional development energies should be placed. Similarly, by studying completed projects, architects and engineers determine how designs for future projects might be improved. In short, in most professional arenas, the person doing the work is also the person assessing the work.

Most public schools, however, are more like assembly lines, for the quality control officer is usually someone above and apart from the teacher. Data on teacher performance are assembled, assessed, and analyzed at levels far removed from the student-teacher interface. A state legislature or a school board often analyzes the previous year's standardized achievement tests and then prescribes an improvement agenda for the state's or district's teachers. Or a principal may reflect on her perceptions of teachers' performance at the school and then prescribe a canned remedy that she thinks is just what the faculty needs.

Most people would agree that no accountability system is as powerful as self-regulation. The standards we set for ourselves are almost always higher than those others would set for us. When we work in systems where others set the standards, we are often inclined to passively resist or to negatively sanction our rate-busting peers.

In the school business, the operative rule is: "He who controls the data controls the agenda." If data on student performance are the property of those outside the classroom, it is those outsiders who determine the pertinent issues and, based on those issues, the further data to be collected. And based on those data, they are free to impose improvement agendas on classroom teachers. Absent any alternative and compelling data of their own, classroom teachers have to bow to the data of their supervisors.

As long as teaching remains a profession where isolation is the norm, where the knowledge that informs practice comes from outside the classroom, and where the quality control officers are removed from the classroom, teaching will be more like a blue-collar job than an intellectual professional pursuit. Eliminating these destructive features is essential to the health of the profession and the success of our schools. By changing the role of teachers, we can also profoundly change the teaching and learning process in our schools. This is not mere speculation. Judith Warren Little (1982) examined instructionally effective schools and found that certain cultural norms tend to prevail. For example, in the most successful schools, teachers are more likely to discuss teaching and learning with one another, to critique each other's work, to collaborate on the preparation of materials, and to jointly design lessons. Little concluded that the norms of collegiality and experimentation were essential ingredients of the work culture of an effective school.

Jon Saphier and Matthew King (1985), summarizing the research on effective school cultures, list twelve norms that distinguish schools where student growth and development are more likely to occur:

1. Collegiality
2. Experimentation
3. High expectations
4. Trust and confidence
5. Tangible support
6. Reaching out to the knowledge bases
7. Appreciation and recognition
8. Caring, celebration, and humor
9. Involvement in decision making
10. Protection of what's important
11. Traditions
12. Honest, open communication

Now we come to the second question posed at the beginning of this chapter: How does collaborative action research fit in? The collaborative action research process outlined in this book is a proven way to foster the very norms that Little and Saphier and King found to be characteristic of effective schools, and that I have shown to be characteristic of most professional occupations. In essence, collaborative action research is a process that enables teachers to improve the teaching-learning process while also contributing to the development of their own profession.

2
Defining Collaborative Action Research

WE CAN BEST UNDERSTAND THE PROCESS OF COLLABORATIVE ACTION research by examining the meaning behind each of the three words used to identify it. Let's begin with the word "action," because action is what distinguishes collaborative action research from the research that most of us have experienced in the past.

The Meaning of "Action"

Traditionally, scientific research has been conducted by professional full-time researchers. They generally choose their topics based on their personal predilections or the preference of journal editors, and they publish reports of their work with the hope that someone will someday make use of it. But even if no one does, their work is usually complete upon publication of their report.

Action research, on the other hand, is conducted by people who want to do something to improve *their own situation*. When other people read about their work, notice it, or make use of it, that is simply icing on the cake. Action researchers undertake a study because they want to know whether they can do something in a better way.

I like to think of scientific researchers as being very much like investigative journalists. They look at what *others* are doing or should be doing. Action researchers, on the other hand, look at what *they themselves* are or should be doing.

Action researchers in education often focus on three related stages of action:

1. Initiating action, such as, adopting a text, choosing an alternative assessment strategy.

2. Monitoring and adjusting action, such as, seeing how a pilot project is proceeding, assessing the early progress of a new program, improving a current practice.

3. Evaluating action, such as, preparing a final report on a completed project.

When we conduct an inquiry for the purpose of initiating action, we are usually seeking information that will help us understand and solve a problem; thus we might call this type of action research "research *for* action." Similarly, when we actually monitor our work so that we can improve our performance, we are engaging in what might be called "research *in* action." Finally, our efforts to evaluate work that has been concluded might be called "research *of* action." Figure 2.1 illustrates what my colleague Peter Holly calls "the three ways into action research."

Figure 2.1
Entry Points for Action Research

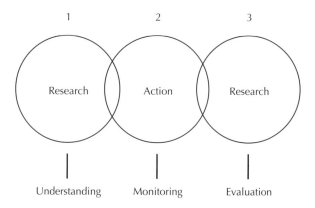

The Meaning of "Research"

Research is defined here as any effort toward disciplined inquiry. Many of us have been schooled in the notion that only investigations that can be reduced to numbers qualify as research. As you will see later in this book, action research can involve a wide array of methods derived from both the quantitative and qualitative domains. In any kind of research, however, there are phenomena researchers want to better understand; therefore they employ systematic processes to acquire valid and reliable data concerning those phenomena.

In the collaborative action research process, the focus of the research is defined by the practitioners themselves. Only two guidelines must be followed: (1) the phenomena chosen for study must concern the teaching/learning process, and (2) those phenomena must also be within the practitioner's scope of influence.

The Meaning of "Collaborative"

Nothing should deter anyone from working alone on research. In fact, most teachers who have undertaken action research have worked alone. As a student teacher, for example, you probably reflected on the design and execution of the first lesson you taught. This is classical action research. First, you approached the lesson with a hypothesis on how best to teach some particular material to a specific group of children. Then you collected data. For instance, as you taught the lesson, you watched students' faces for clues about how well your lesson was being received, and during independent practice, you walked around the room to see how students were progressing. You probably also reviewed students' tests or quizzes to ascertain what they learned. Finally, you concluded your research by evaluating all these data and drawing conclusions about how you might teach this material differently, should the opportunity present itself.

The above example contains almost all the elements of a full action research study, minus a plan to write up and share the results. Undoubtedly, if we had continued to use this type of disciplined inquiry throughout our teaching careers, we would all probably have become more thoughtful teachers and better educators, yet we would still have been working in isolation. By turning to *collaborative* action research, however, we can renew our commitment to thoughtful teaching and also begin developing an active community of professionals. The process described in this book is based on teams of practitioners who have common interests and work together to investigate issues related to those interests.

An Overview of the Five-step Process

The process of collaborative action research has five sequential steps:

1. Problem formulation
2. Data collection
3. Data analysis
4. Reporting of results
5. Action planning

1. Problem Formulation

This step, which is described in detail in Chapter 3, helps action researchers identify the issues that are of the greatest professional concern. Researchers identify what they already know about each issue, what they still need to know about it, and their understanding of the variables affecting the issue.

2. Data Collection

Data collection is the heart of the five-step process. The credibility of any research effort lives or dies on the quality of the data used to support its conclusions. To ensure adequate data collection, action researchers, their colleagues, students, and any other persons involved in the research are expected to assemble three sets of data for each research question that surfaced during the problem formulation phase. This second step of the collaborative action research process is looked at more closely in Chapter 4.

3. Data Analysis

If data collection is the heart of the research process, then data analysis is its soul. Most action researchers find this step to be the most enjoyable of the entire process. It involves looking systematically at all the data collected to see what trends or patterns emerge and what conclusions, if any, can be drawn. Chapter 5 explores the data analysis process.

4. Reporting Results

Inviting others to peer over our shoulders and learn from our practice is one of the most powerful and rewarding aspects of collaborative action research. Thus, it is imperative that teams of action researchers find as many appropriate forums as possible to share what they are learning about teaching and learning. Chapter 6 describes several ways to share what has been learned and expand the ring of collegiality.

5. Action Planning

Since the purpose of collaborative action research is to improve our professional practice, the process won't be complete until we have put in place plans incorporating what we've learned as a result of our systematic inquiry. Chapter 7 discusses several processes for using the findings of collaborative action research to plan and implement school and classroom improvement.

* * *

Now that we've looked briefly at the process, we can examine each step in depth.

3
Problem Formulation

THE TIME DEMANDS OF INSTRUCTION, INSERVICE TRAINING, AND program improvement leave little time for the reflection necessary to develop a truly meaningful research question. Yet it is essential that collaborative action researchers have sufficient time to accomplish this crucial step. Our experience has shown that teachers who rush to complete the problem formulation stage are more likely to flounder in their later efforts, whereas teachers who take time to reflect on and define their problem are more likely to pursue questions yielding meaningful results.

In this chapter, I describe a series of techniques that have been used successfully to help beginning action researchers sharpen their focus on a research topic of significant concern to them. It is not important for teachers to come to this process with a problem in mind. The only prerequisite for participating in collaborative action research is a sincere desire to work with colleagues to improve teaching and learning.

Reflective Interviewing

The technique of reflective interviewing requires about an hour of uninterrupted time. It is often used in departmental or grade-level meetings or during scheduled faculty meetings. After a brief introduction, each participant is asked to choose a partner who will assist her in talking about an issue that meets the following guidelines:

- The issue involves teaching and learning.
- The issue is something I can influence.
- The issue is something I'm deeply concerned about.

One partner interviews the other for twenty to thirty minutes, then the leader of the meeting calls time and the partners reverse roles. It is important that everyone be instructed that they are conducting interviews, not engaging in discussions. The key distinction is that in an interview, the person being interviewed has an opportunity to fully and deeply explore feelings and ideas on an issue of personal concern. The interviewer assists by asking clarifying questions and providing needed probes to get over hurdles. Interviewers must be careful not to take over or interfere in the respondent's personal reflection.

Most teachers are natural interviewers who rarely need much training on how to be an effective interviewer and active listener. Some guidelines for interviewers may be useful, however. Here are a few that we have used in our training programs:

1. Make the interview comfortable but challenging.
2. Keep it challenging but not threatening.
3. Try to elicit deep responses.
4. Try to elicit broad responses.
5. Keep the interview somewhat structured, but allow for flexibility and spontaneity.
6. Consider the rights and feelings of the respondent.

The purpose of the reflective interview is to enable teachers to get in touch with those core issues of practice that matter the most to them. Surfacing personal concerns early in the process is important because today's busy teachers are disinclined to invest even small amounts of time and energy on projects or inquiries that seem tangential to their core concerns. Another and perhaps equally important reason for conducting the reflective interview is to emphasize up front that it is the "actor," the teacher, who is driving the collaborative action research process. Even in the best of schools, there is sometimes a suspicion that school improvement initiatives are really elaborate plans drawn up by supervisors to involve the teaching staff in an administrative agenda. Placing teachers' instructional concerns right up front will clearly establish that the collaborative action research process is for the teachers' benefit.

Analytic Discourse

This second technique, which is similar to a group interview, is to be used after the reflective interview. It also requires an uninterrupted period of at least one hour. Engaging in analytic discourse helps teachers more deeply explore their current understanding of the phenomena under discussion. This technique may seem superfluous at first, but once teachers become familiar with it, they rarely abandon it. Beyond its utility in helping teachers more clearly define their issues prior to conducting collaborative action research, analytic discourse can also be institutionalized into *any* work group to enhance collegiality.

The first step in preparing for analytic discourse is to have each action research team sit in a circle and briefly (two or three minutes each) share the issues that surfaced in the reflective interviews. This step enhances communication and allows the team members to see how their personal concerns mesh with the issues troubling their colleagues. If one particular issue emerges as important to most participants, which often happens, then that issue is the logical one to focus on in analytic discourse.

Once all the issues are on the table, each team needs to find a volunteer who is willing to be the subject of a group interview. Participants will later find this role to be a rewarding one, but at first some people may find it to be quite an intimidating prospect. For this reason, no one should be forced into playing the interviewee role.

Once a volunteer has been secured, the team sits in a comfortable arrangement (usually a horseshoe format) to conduct the group interview. Before getting started, the leader explains the purpose of the activity:

> Our purpose is to help Joan come to a full understanding of her knowledge about an issue that is troubling her. Our analytic discourse will be considered complete when Joan is able to say, "That's it, I've fully explained to you what I understand about this issue and all of its parts," and when each of you is able to accurately paraphrase Joan's perspective on this problem.

The leader also tells the team that for analytic discourse to be effective, they *must* adhere to a strict set of rules:

- Interviewers can only *ask* questions.
- Interviewers can make *no* critical comments.
- Interviewers can offer *no* solutions.

After providing forty-five to sixty minutes for the interview, the leader asks the team to discuss their reactions to the activity. Typically, interviewees would be asked:

- How did it feel to be interviewed?
- How did it feel to have the undivided attention of a group of colleagues on a topic you're concerned about?

And interviewers would be asked:

- What was it like to be an interviewer?
- What was it like to restrain yourself from intruding into the discussion and instead try to understand a colleague's issue in all of its complexity?

During this discussion, participants often say that analytic discourse was both a new and invigorating experience for them. It is wonderful that most participants find the experience to be stimulating, but it is disappointing, too, for it indicates that this kind of collegial interaction is rare. Consider for a moment how powerful it would be for teachers to regularly exchange ideas this way at faculty meetings, just as professionals in law offices, architectural firms, and advertising agencies do in their daily or weekly meetings.

Completing an analytic discourse allows the action research team to find out whether its members share an interest in a general topic. If they do, there may be no further need to conduct another analytic discourse—at least not for purposes of problem identification. If the interests of the team members seem to be divergent, however, everyone should be given an opportunity to participate in the deep reflection that this process provides.

Having now spent several hours verbally reflecting on issues of deep professional concern, the action research teams will be getting a clear picture of their problem areas, at least as far as they currently understand them.

Infrequently, two things happen simultaneously at this point. First, team members begin to develop a precise description of the current situation. For example, they might agree that:

• Students are experiencing difficulties in recalling main ideas from their reading, or

• Teachers are seeing a decline in self-esteem as students move up the grades, or

• Students are failing to complete their assignments successfully.

It is also common for action researchers to have already begun to develop some ideas for attacking the identified problem. This is one of the glorious, albeit untidy, differences between action research and traditional research. Scientists, divorced from the role of actor, simply describe the current situation; action researchers, compelled by their desire for improved actions, will be reluctant to deprive their students of the possible benefits of their developing insights. For this reason, interventions frequently come to the surface throughout the process, perhaps even before the description phase has been completed.

In the scientific community, taking action on incomplete data is often considered inappropriate; for example, in pharmaceutical research, even the most promising cures are often held back until the experimental trials have been thoroughly analyzed. No similar regulations exist in action research, and if they did, enforcing them would be difficult, for teacher-researchers have strong commitments to their students that will always push them to act rather than wait for more data.

Graphic Representation

The graphic representation is a technique that invites action researchers to move their thinking from the left side of the brain to the right. It provides an opportunity for teacher-researchers to actually draw a picture of the phenomena under study, including all the factors thought to be influencing the phenomena, as well as proposed solutions that have surfaced. The purpose of this technique is to allow the relationships between factors, variables, and contexts to be looked at in a fresh light and then debated. The graphic representation technique has four steps:

Step 1. Brainstorm all the relevant factors, variables, and contexts. The workshop leader should supply each team with a large sheet of paper (minimum 2' X 3'), a pad of Post-it notes, pencils, and colored felt-tip markers. Then team members should be asked to list every relevant theme, idea, issue, factor, or variable that arose during their reflective interviews, their analytic discourses, or other discussions of the problem area. Each factor should be written on a separate Post-it note. For example, if the team had been discussing the drop in student self-esteem, the factors listed might be: grading practices, tracking, retention, parental support, teachers' collaborative action research, peer pressure, drug abuse, cooperative classrooms, competitive classrooms, school activities, socioeconomic status, and cliques.

Step 2. Arrange relevant factors, variables, and contexts in relational order. Once the team members have brainstormed and written all of the issues or factors they believe pertain to the problem, they gather around the paper and as a group attempt to arrange the issues on the Post-it notes in a logical pattern. As the team begins trying to illustrate their common understandings of the relationships between factors, the shortcomings of a verbal process often become apparent, and debates invariably ensue. For example, one person might say that he thinks school activities enhance students' self-esteem, while another person asserts the contrary, arguing that only students with high self-esteem participate in school activities. Suddenly, a group of people that seemed to be of one mind begins to realize that individual team members are seeing the issue in somewhat different ways.

It will take time for team members to reach consensus, usually at least an hour. The virtue of the Post-it notes is that no arrangement is permanent; emerging hypotheses and theories can easily be changed by simply moving the notes.

Once the team members have achieved some degree of consensus on the relationships between the issues, it's time to take out the colored markers and, using lines, arrows, and symbols, draw the relationships. Figure 3.1 illustrates a portion of a graphic representation done by a high school team concerned about the paucity of problem-solving strategies being demonstrated by their students. Figure 3.2 shows the way the team thought they could go about solving the problem. Superimposing the second graphic representation on top of the first produces a new graphic showing teachers' complete view of the issue (see Figure 3.3).

Once they have drawn a full picture, teachers usually feel some satisfaction because they have made clear their common understandings and acknowledged their shared viewpoints. Team members feel as though they are of one mind. But what if they are wrong? What if their presumed understanding of the issue is flawed? These are important questions because when teachers or other professionals embark on improvement projects based on hypotheses that may be wrong, the solutions they attempt are likely to fail, and failure reduces feelings of personal and professional efficacy. Most educators have too many memories of seductive innovations that were built on false assumptions and demanded a lot of time, enthusiasm, and commitment, yet brought only failure and deep and profound disillusionment. As a result, our schools are filled with teachers who often seem unwilling to try anything new because, as they say, "We've been through all this before." Encouraging teachers to come up with an accurate picture of the current situation as they currently understand it is a good way to overcome this attitude. It gives teachers themselves the responsibility for change. But this is only one step in the process.

Step 3. Evaluate our knowledge base. Up to this point, the collaborative action research process has been built from the knowledge, background, and perspective that team members brought to the instructional problem. The suggested activities simply helped the team clarify their previous understandings in all of their depth and breadth. It would be wrong to stop there, however, because few of us are prepared to say that we already have all the answers to the many truly perplexing educational problems. After all, if we did have the answers, the issues would hardly be perplexing!

Figure 3.1
Graphic Representation of a Problem Area

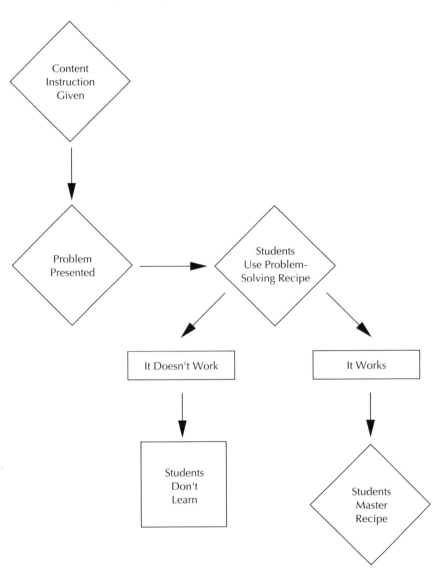

Figure 3.2
Graphic Representation of Proposed Intervention

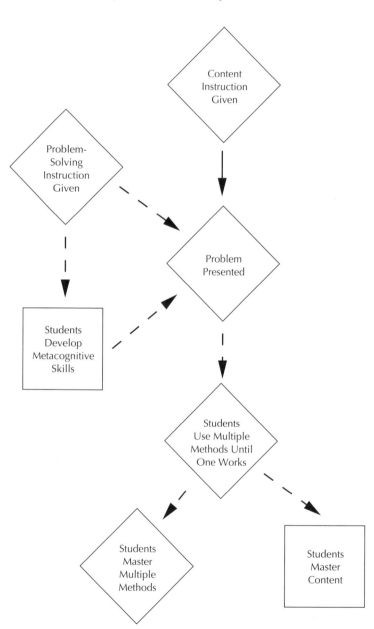

Figure 3.3
Graphic Reconstruction

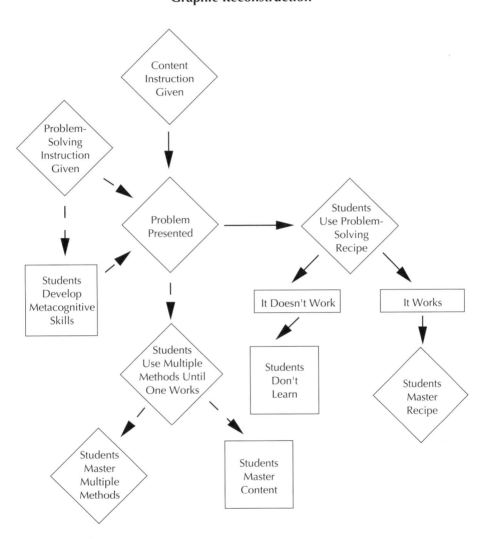

In the third step of the graphic representation, teachers analyze their picture with a critical eye and ask themselves, "Are we sure about this?" More specifically, they ask:

• Are the relationships between the variables or factors what we think they are?

• Are there other variables or issues that should be considered?

• Are we forgetting something?

First, the team looks at each line or arrow in the graphic representation, keeping in mind that each arrow is an assumption about a relationship. The team asks these questions about each presumed relationship:

• Do we know this to be true?

• What evidence leads us to that conclusion?

• What if our assumption is incorrect? How does it alter our understanding of the issue?

There will be many relationships on our graphic representation that we will know to be true. The basis for this knowledge could be prior research, professional experience, or research data we recently collected. The relationships we *know* to exist need not be the subject of any further investigation. For example, we might choose to accept as a given that there is a relationship between poor grades and the likelihood of dropping out of school, or a relationship between enjoying school and truancy. If, however, we find we have no empirical basis for supporting our current assumptions about an important relationship shown in our graphic representation, then we will want to collect some valid and reliable data to establish the actual existence of the relationship.

In fact, all the relationships we aren't fairly certain of should be investigated further unless the relationship itself is deemed irrelevant. For example, let's say we had inferred that possessing brown eyes was a factor that made a child less likely to drop out. We might well conclude that we had no evidence to support that assumption; yet we might also conclude that it wasn't worth trying to confirm or disconfirm, because altering children's eye color is impossible.

After completing a team analysis of all the lines and arrows in the graphic representation, it should be clear where additional data are needed to make the graphic representation accurately reflect reality. It's important to use some kind of identifier to distinguish between the representations the team is sure of and those that require further investigation. For instance, I use dotted lines to show relationships about which I'm uncertain. If I'm confident of the relationship, I make the line solid.

4. Surfacing the research questions. Those relationships that the team concluded were meaningful, yet still need to be verified, become the focus of the research project. It is helpful to translate these relationships into questions. For example, the team might want to know:

• What student attributes contribute to student success with spelling?

• What contributes to making a parent conference worthwhile?

• Do all children benefit equally from cooperative learning in math?

Once the key research questions have been formed and agreed to by the team, only one small step remains before moving into the data collection process: writing the problem statement.

The Problem Statement

In our investigations of the factors contributing to the successful completion of collaborative action research projects, the variable of "focus" was among the most significant. Teams who began their work with a clear idea of what they were studying and why they were studying it tended to find the motivation to complete their work. Conversely, the teams who lacked clarity on what they were about tended to lose interest in their collaborative work. Therefore, we recommend that collaborative action research teams complete the problem identification process by composing a problem statement of approximately 100 words that clearly and concisely answers the following questions:

1. Who is affected?
2. Who or what is suspected of causing the problem?

3. What kind of problem is it? (e.g., a problem with goals, skills, resources, time, etc.)
4. What is the goal for improvement?
5. What do we propose to do about it? (optional)

Figures 3.4 and 3.5 show sample problem statements that answer these questions.

Figure 3.4
Research Problem Statement

- Students at Sunset High School appear to have a limited repertoire of learning strategies. [This answers questions 1 and 3].

- We suspect that this is a result of inadequate direct instruction in learning skills. [This answers question 2.]

- We want all Sunset students to be able to use and articulate multiple learning strategies when approaching academic tasks. [This answers question 4.]

- To accomplish this, we will infuse instruction in metacognition into each academic discipline. [This answers question 5.]

Research Questions:

1. Will instruction in metacognition improve students' ability to articulate and use multiple learning strategies with their school work?

2. What contributes to the effectiveness of content in teaching metacognition?

3. How does instruction in metacognition affect student attitudes and performance?

Figure 3.5
Research Problem Statement

- Students at Highland Elementary School aren't seeing the connections between their school subjects. [This answers questions 1 and 3.]

- The action research group believes this is a result of our schedule and the way we teach the different subjects. [This answers question 2.]

- We want all our students to see the relevance of the school curriculum, to appreciate the relationship between the academic disciplines, and to be able to apply the skills learned in one subject to problem solving in another. [This answers question 4.]

- Therefore, we plan to integrate our instruction from science, math, language arts, and social studies into interdisciplinary units on society and technology. [This answers question 5.]

Research Questions:

1. What difficulties do students have translating skills from subject to subject?

2. Do students transfer skills more readily between subjects they enjoy?

3. What leads to students' enjoying a subject?

4. What is the difference between achievement in multidisciplinary classes and in single-subject classes?

A Reality Check_____

The next chapter will deal with the second component of the collaborative action research process, planning and carrying out data collection. Before embarking on those tasks (which are the heart of the research process), each team member should pause to answer these four questions:

1. Is our research tied to what I have to do or want to do? If the answer is no, change topics. As a busy teacher, you should commit to work only on what you consider a priority.

2. Is our research focused? In other words, are you clear on what this investigation is about and why it's being conducted? If not, stop until you get that clarity. You don't want to wander aimlessly.

3. How involved do you want to be in this research project? You need to be prepared to tell your partners what they can and cannot expect from you as the project proceeds.

4. What will be the basis for team sharing? Earlier in this book, we discussed the value of collaborative professional work. We all gain more, learn more, and are more professionally satisfied when we work with others. Nevertheless, the collaborative action research process described in this book is based on each professional working on personal priorities. What do you do when these two principles appear to be in conflict? The answer lies in the nature of your team and the issues the members want to investigate. Assume, for example, that you have joined a team of teachers who share some particular interest. For some reason, however, you find you don't enjoy working with the team. In this case, you would probably have trouble finding a basis for sharing, and should instead pursue individual action research or join another collegial group whose members seem to truly enjoy working together. People who enjoy working together can usually find some basis for sharing, though the level of sharing may be low or high, as shown on the following continuum.

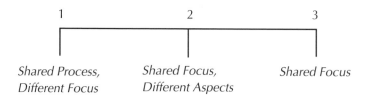

1	2	3
Shared Process, Different Focus	*Shared Focus, Different Aspects*	*Shared Focus*

A team that finds itself at point 3 on the continuum is one where everyone is interested in the same issues and has decided to pursue their common interests by engaging in a single action research project. Examples might include a team of English teachers examining the effects of peer editing on the quality of student writing, or a 4th grade team investigating the effects of a multidisciplinary unit.

Another team might find itself at point 2. Here everyone is interested in the same general focus area, but each member finds that she has a passion for different aspects of that focus. An example could be the school in which all ten members of an action research team are interested in the multi-age grouping process being introduced at the school; however, each teacher is intrigued by a different aspect or issue related to multi-age grouping. Another example might be the middle school faculty that wants to investigate cooperative learning, although one member wants to investigate its effects on self-esteem while another wants to find out how it affects teacher preparation time and stress, and still another wants to see how it might affect students' attainment of thinking skills. These teams would do well to conduct multiple projects and meet regularly to share what they are learning about their common interest areas.

Finally, it is possible that a team will find itself at point 1. Here everyone has caught the action research bug and is eager to pursue an inquiry, but all the focuses are idiosyncratic. Diverse focuses should not be cause for concern. Many such teams have constituted themselves as action research support groups that meet every two weeks simply to share what they have been learning. What these teams have in common is a commitment to the action research process, and what they receive from each other is procedural help, as well as the active listening of caring and concerned peers.

As a result of reflecting on a problem area and analyzing what they know about it, team members should be able to identify gaps in their knowledge base. The next step is to fill in those gaps.

4
Data Collection

THE GUIDING PRINCIPLE BEHIND THE DATA COLLECTION PROCESS IS
that the information collected should be compelling enough
to convince any skeptic. Although the primary audience for
action research is the action research team itself, a team
sometimes needs to win the support of resident skeptics or
cynics in the school; skeptics or cynics usually need
overwhelming data to convince them of anything. And in
most school districts, conservative pockets in the hierarchy
will resist changes in program direction whenever possible.
Collecting data that are valid enough to allay concerns (or
to at least create cognitive dissonance for the resisters) is
the main function of the data collection process.

Three Important Qualities

Researchers have traditionally been concerned with
three qualities of their results: validity, reliability, and
generalizability. Before we discuss the data collection
process any further, let's briefly consider each of these
qualities.

Generalizability

Generalizability refers to the applicability of findings to
settings and contexts different from the one in which they
were originally obtained. Historically, many educational
researchers have tried to avoid research that might lead to
findings that could be attacked as being too limited in scope
or specific only to a certain context. Instead, they have
sought to identify factors that apply in many contexts. For
instance, the work on teaching effectiveness done by David

Berliner, Madeline Hunter, and others sought to identify those general factors of instruction and lesson design that were applicable across all subjects, grade levels, and categories of students. Similarly, the work on effective schooling sought to find those general characteristics of schools that correlated with effectiveness regardless of the unique attributes of the communities in which they developed.

It is true that much good has come from such work, but its limitations are obvious to any classroom teacher. One reason most teachers are skeptical of this type of research is that they intuitively sense the powerful pull of context. After all, teachers know that what worked with their third period class may well fail with their sixth period class, even though both groups of students are using the same materials. If an idea that worked with one group of students at 10:00 a.m. can't be guaranteed to work with another group of students from the same school at 2:00 p.m., then classroom context must be an important factor. Action researchers certainly think so. Instead of attempting to compensate for context, as scientific researchers do, action researchers embrace context as an integral part of their work.

As action researchers, you don't need to worry about the generalizability of your data because you are not seeking to define the ultimate truths of learning theory. Your goal is to understand what is happening in your school or classroom and to determine what might improve things in that context. Although it is important for you to understand and explain the intricacies of the local context, it is not your mission to declare your context as either typical or atypical. That is a decision to be made by others who observe your work or read about it. For example, in his book *Among Schoolchildren,* Tracy Kidder (1989) does not attempt to argue that "Ms. Jones" is a typical 2nd grade teacher. Instead, he leaves it to his readers to decide whether the teacher's experiences relate to their situations. Likewise, individual readers must decide whether the suffering of Hamlet is unique to his circumstances or is shared by the whole of the human race. Shakespeare, like the action researcher, leaves judgments about generalizability up to the reader.

The other two quality issues involving your results,

validity and reliability, are as applicable to collaborative action research as they are to traditional research studies.

Validity

The concept of validity is found in the question "Do these data really measure or represent what we say they do?" This is a crucial issue. Superstition, bad practice, and even malpractice could be the result of action taken on the basis of invalid data. In *The Mismeasure of Man,* Stephen Jay Gould (1981) points out that not long ago, the pseudo-science of phrenology was accepted as valid practice. Phrenologists held that the size and shape of a person's skull were an indicator of the intellectual capacity and character of that person. If our schools were still influenced by the invalid assumptions of the phrenologists, students with large hat sizes would be assigned to the gifted program, while students with small hat sizes would be assigned to special education courses. Such an outcome would be humorous were it not for the fact that it actually happened. The consequences for students are real and severe when important educational decisions are based on invalid instrumentation, data, or theories. For this reason, as action researchers, we should always strive to be able to defend our findings and reports as valid, meaning they measure what they claim to measure.

Reliability

Reliability concerns the accuracy of your methods of measurement. If each subsequent administration of a particular instrument produces wildly different results, then the instrument is deemed to be unreliable. For instance, as teachers, we are familiar with the practice of using standardized achievement tests to reliably measure the performance of a large group of students. The aggregate score posted by a group of students at a large school on a test given last Tuesday won't differ significantly from the aggregate score posted by the same students on the same test given the following Wednesday. Standardized tests are, however, grossly unreliable in their characterization of the abilities of *individual* students. On most norm-referenced tests, a student's score could differ by as much as 30 percentile points from one administration to the next. The difference here is so extreme that a student could be labeled gifted one week and learning-disabled the next. Clearly, the consequences of making programmatic decisions based on unreliable data (i.e., data that are the results of an instrument with a high margin of error) are quite serious.

Action research teams should begin their planning for data collection guided by three questions:

• Do the instruments and methods we plan to use measure what we claim they do?

• Do the instruments and methods we plan to use accurately measure the phenomena we are studying?

• Will a skeptic be convinced by the weight of the data we amass?

We will be returning to how collaborative action researchers satisfy themselves on these three fronts later in this chapter. Let's look now at some of the data collection options available to your team.

Sources of Data

One of the factors that has limited the collection of data for school and classroom decision making is the belief that good data are both difficult and expensive to collect. Many of us have been led to believe that only data obtained with highly technical instrumentation can yield valid results. The experience of hundreds of action researchers, however, has demonstrated that these beliefs do not reflect reality; schools are naturally data-rich environments, and simply opening our eyes to some of the most frequently used and easily obtainable sources of data can make planning the data collection process much easier. Remember that there is no one correct source of data for school-based action research. The best source will be determined by the research questions your team is asking. Here are some of the more common sources of data:

• *Existing Sources*
  – Student work (portfolios)
  – Archival evidence

- *Tools for Capturing Everyday Life*
  – Diaries, logs, journals
  – Videos
  – Photographs
  – Shadowing
  – Observational checklists/rating scales
- *Tools for Questioning*
  – Interviews
  – Written Surveys
  – Tests

As you can see, the data sources are listed under three categories. The items in the first category are data that already exist in every school and classroom. To use this information in your action research, all you need is permission to use it, a way to access it and save it, and a way to sort it that will give it meaning. The items in the second category are all tools for capturing the richness and texture of the everyday life of schools and classrooms. Finally, the items in the third category are questioning tools that will require the development or acquisition of instrumentation. I will discuss each of these three categories separately and elaborate on a few of the more commonly used sources of data.

Existing Sources

The files in the office of every school in America contain data on student attendance, family background, standardized achievement scores, disciplinary referrals, grades, and previous schools attended for nearly all students. These files can often provide answers to our questions about patterns in the behavior and academic performance of students. Getting at the data may take time, and organizing such information is often hard work. Administrators can provide valuable support for school-based action research teams by supplying clerical help to assemble and sort the data.

In one school where I worked, we conducted an academic post mortem of a class that had graduated the previous spring. We first divided the class into four achievement groups (based upon the quartile of their 9th grade standardized achievement tests). We then proceeded to compare these four groups based on gender, courses taken, special services used, number of years in the system, grades earned, extracurricular activities, disciplinary incidents, attendance, post–high school work or education placement, and 12th grade standardized achievement scores. From this study, we developed a clear picture of the academic careers of four (and when divided by gender, eight) different categories of students. We were able to understood more about our grading patterns, our disciplinary practices, the success or lack of success of our Chapter I and special education programs, the reach of our activities and athletic programs, and our grouping practices. Remarkably, all of this was accomplished without contacting a single student; all the data we needed were in the files, thus, a few hours of secretarial time provided the faculty with mounds of useful data on which we could base our school improvement efforts.

Another type of readily available data is students' work. The value of maintaining student portfolios has been discussed by many educators, and the practice has much to commend it. One of the side benefits of the use of portfolios is that it gives teacher-researchers ready access to meaningful longitudinal data on student growth and development. Anyone who has viewed old home movies or paged through a well-maintained baby album can understand the significance of being able to examine various stages of development. When teachers want to quantify the results of student growth, they can simply ask teachers of similar subjects and grade levels to score pieces of students' work done throughout the semester or year. The identity of students is usually kept from the scorers, and each student work is scored by two or three teachers to ensure the reliability of the findings.

Tools for Capturing Everyday Life

Often the questions or issues for which we need to acquire data call for us to take a critical look at exactly how we are spending our time. But how do we find ways to step back and look objectively at ourselves? Many people believe that this outside-looking-in perspective can be obtained only by using an outside investigator. Not so! Action researchers have within themselves many of the means necessary to take a fresh look at the world they are immersed in. Here are some examples:

Journals. Suppose that twenty teachers in an elementary school have decided to implement whole-language instruction. The faculty wants to examine the implementation issues involved in establishing this program. Now imagine that every teacher agrees to spend only ten minutes every day (immediately after the children leave) for three weeks writing in a journal responses to this prompt: "Describe what went well, what went poorly, or what was a surprise for you today during language arts instruction."

It's unlikely that anyone would be overburdened by an additional ten minutes per day given to personal reflection, yet in just two weeks the teachers would have 280 separate journal entries that could be discussed and analyzed by the team. This is an example of a small investment producing a treasure trove for an action research team.

Videotape and Photography. Videotape and photography may at first strike you as being too subjective a way to capture the reality of daily life. If you reflect further, however, I think you'll find that this is not necessarily so. If you have ever looked at books of photo essays about countries, regions, or national parks or paged through a truly inspired high school yearbook, you have probably said to yourself, "Yes, that *is* what it's like." Well-chosen photos and videos can portray the textures and realities of schools and classrooms in a vivid light. Conversely, they can also be used to distort reality. Later in this chapter, however, we will discuss triangulation, which is the action researcher's chief protection against allowing one distortion to slant an entire research project.

Shadowing. Shadowing is a tool that can help us see people and circumstances as they really are. It gives us an opportunity to experience a situation in a most naturalistic manner. With school-based action research, the shadowing process involves following selected students or teachers for a specified period of time (generally a day) to collect a picture of a typical day in their life. At a high school where I worked, we conducted such self-examinations annually. Twelve teachers shadowed twelve students (three from each grade level, including a high-, middle-, and low-achieving student from each grade) for one day each. At the end of the twelve-day shadowing period, the students and their shadows met to compare notes. Ultimately, the twenty-four participants (shadows and shadowees) met with the entire faculty to discuss similarities and differences in the way students of different ages and performance levels experienced our school. (A more detailed description of this process can be found in Sagor 1981.)

Checklists and Rating Scales. Checklists and rating scales require less work than shadowing, yet they can still yield rich data for analysis. The checklist/rating scale process involves three steps:

1. Agree on what constitutes a particular behavior or category.
2. Visit classrooms to collect data.
3. Arrange the data into categories.

With the checklist process, one or two people can collect all the data, thereby saving time for the team, yet enabling everyone to have faith in the data. The key is to have prior agreement on the criteria used for rating. Figures 4.1 and 4.2 on the next two pages show data obtained through checklists from an observer who took readings on student and teacher behavior every thirty seconds. This research was conducted to assess the schoolwide use of class time by students and teachers.

Figure 4.3 on page 38 reflects the results of a series of classroom observations lasting ten minutes each. The observers focused on trying to categorize the cognitive level of the instructional activities pursued.

These uses of checklists provided vivid portraits of how class time and activities were being used. Although the data collection involved only one collector, the data were available to everyone in the action research teams.

Tools for Questioning

Often the information we are looking for isn't immediately available through simple observation, so we have to delve into what people know, believe, or feel about an issue. In such cases, we are inclined to collect data through the use of tests, surveys, and interviews.

Tests. Tests are generally used to ascertain levels of

Figure 4.1
632 Snapshots of Teacher Activities

Activity	No. of snapshots where observed	Percentage of total snapshots*
Responding to or helping individual students	112	17%
Asking questions	100	15%
Lecturing	91	14%
Paperwork (at desk)	42	7%
Active monitoring (looking for students needing help)	41	6%
Getting materials	38	6%
Administering tests (proctoring)	27	4%
Management (attendance, organizational details)	27	4%
Audio-visual equipment set-up	25	4%
Observing student performance	23	4%
Responding to student questions	20	3%
Absent from room	16	3%
Giving directions on an assignment	12	2%
Demonstrating for students	11	2%
Cleaning up after lab	9	1%
Small-group instruction	8	1%
Correcting homework	5	1%
Listening to recitations	5	1%
Miscellaneous	5	1%
Admonishing student(s)	5	1%
Waiting for attention	2	.3%
Monitoring student behavior	2	.3%
Calling on a student	2	.3%
Discussion	2	.3%
Dealing with interruptions	1	.2%
Social Interaction with students	1	.2%

*Note: Due to rounding off, these percentages do not total 100 percent.

Figure 4.2
643 Snapshots of Student Activities

Activity	No. of snapshots where observed	Percentage of total snapshots
Seatwork	142	22%
Listening to teacher	112	17%
Responding to questions from teacher	91	14%
Lab work	88	14%
Taking tests	65	10%
Visiting with each other	25	4%
Performing	18	3%
Reciting	14	2%
Asking the teacher questions	14	2%
Watching or listening to to audio-visual materials	13	2%
Getting out materials	12	2%
Group work	10	2%
Clean-up	10	2%
Observing performance	8	1%
Discussion	8	1%
Responding to questions in writing	5	.8%
Responding to management questions	4	.6%
Observing teacher demonstrations	2	.3%
Waiting	2	.3%

Figure 4.3
Types of Cognitive Activities Observed
in a Series of Classroom Observations

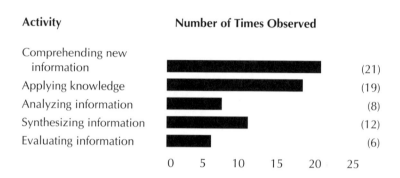

Activity	Number of Times Observed	
Comprehending new information		(21)
Applying knowledge		(19)
Analyzing information		(8)
Synthesizing information		(12)
Evaluating information		(6)

0   5   10   15   20   25

skill and knowledge. Action research teams can take advantage of already-developed tests, norm-referenced standardized tests, criterion-referenced tests, Regents' exams, or tests developed by textbook publishers. Occasionally teams may want to develop tests of their own. Because of the importance of obtaining valid, reliable data, it is generally a good idea to consult with a critical friend before administering a test as part of an action research project (the role of the critical friend will be discussed at the end of this chapter).

Written Surveys. Written surveys are favorite data-gathering techniques for action researchers because they enable us to get at emotional, cognitive, and attitudinal issues. Here are some guidelines for developing surveys:

• Surveys can be used to gather data concerning affective, cognitive, or attitudinal issues, depending on how we frame the questions. For example, we might ask questions like:

    a. What are our current school goals? (cognitive)
    b. What is your opinion of the quality of our school goals? (attitudinal)
    c. How do you feel about working on our school goals? (affective)

• Strive for clarity. Conduct a small field test to make sure participants will understand your survey questions.

• Strive for brevity. Surveys should take no longer than ten minutes to administer.

• Provide an opportunity for participants to make additional comments.

• Consider disaggregation and confidentiality issues in advance.

• Remember that your first goal is face validity. Will a skeptic believe your results?

• Avoid suggesting a desired response (asking "leading questions"). For example, instead of asking, "What is the effect of tardiness on achievement?" ask, "What factors influence achievement in our school?" or "What is the effect of tardiness in our school?"

• Try to separate fact from opinion by asking follow-up questions like "How do you know? or "What led you to this opinion?"

• When using numerical scales, ask for an explanation of responses. For example:

How would you rate discipline in this school?

Poor		Average		Excellent
1	2	3	4	5

What would it take to make your rating a five?

• When using numerical scales, consider whether you want a scale that forces people to respond either positively or negatively (an even-numbered scale) or a scale that allows people to respond neutrally (an odd-numbered scale).

• Finally, remember that when you collect data from people, you must be willing to share with them your results.

Interviews. When using interviews to collect data, it is helpful to work from an interview guide, which is simply a general road map to help the interviewer direct the discussion in a manner that is likely to produce relevant information and insights. Although an interview usually requires considerable time commitments from both interviewer and interviewee, it is an excellent way to collect data. Most people enjoy being interviewed because your interest tells them you really care what they think;

nevertheless, their time must be respected. For this reason, you should avoid the need for follow-up interviews. You can do so by using the interview guide to keep yourself on track. Here are some basic points to consider when developing your guide (note that these guidelines are very similar to those for developing surveys):

• Limit yourself to ten to fifteen question areas.

• Reread the research questions the team developed in the problem formulation stage before writing the first draft of the guide.

• Review the research questions after writing the guide to be sure you have asked for all relevant information.

• Follow all your factual and opinion questions with "why" probes.

• Decide how the interview data will be collected: through videotape or audiotape, your notes, or the notes of a co-interviewer.

• Remember that interviews may be used to obtain cognitive, opinion, and affective data. For example, you might ask:

– What do you recall about our current school goals? (cognitive)
– What is your opinion of the quality of our school goals? (opinion)
– How do you feel about working on our school goals? (affective)

• Strive for clarity. Practice your interview with a friend.

• Strive for brevity. An interview should last no longer than forty-five minutes.

• Provide an opportunity for respondents to give full explanations.

• Consider disaggregation and confidentiality issues in advance.

• Avoid suggesting a desired response through a leading question. For example, instead of asking, "What is the effect of tardiness on achievement?" ask "What factors influence achievement in our school?" or "What is the effect of tardiness in our school?"

• Try to separate fact from opinion by asking follow-up questions like these: "How do you know?" "What led you to this opinion?"

• When using numerical scales, always ask for an explanation of responses. For example:

How would you rate discipline in this school?

Poor		Average		Excellent
1	2	3	4	5

What would it take to make your rating a five?

The best aspect of interviews and surveys is that they provide us with actual voices and precise words. Later, when we report our data, this type of information can add credibility to our reports and vitality to our findings. On occasion, however, action researchers have found themselves in trouble by not considering a few basic issues before using these questioning methods. The three most important issues to consider before embarking on data solicitation are confidentiality, disaggregation, and reporting back.

Confidentiality/anonymity. One reason for collecting data through open-ended surveys or interviews is to capture the precise words of your subjects. Before you collect this information, however, you will need to have thought through exactly how you intend to make use of the data obtained. Do you intend to quote sources by name or will you hide their identity? Is it possible to shield identities, or will a careful reader be able to puncture your shroud of secrecy? At the start of any interview or survey, you will want to tell your subject(s) how the data will be used and what confidentiality (if any) will be maintained. Having given these assurances, you *must* maintain them, for your integrity and the opportunities for other action researchers following you depend on your doing so.

A second and related issue involving surveys is whether the individual subjects will be (or need to be) anonymous to the researchers. There is much debate on this topic. Some researchers believe that the freedom to speak anonymously encourages honest and open responses. Others feel that it invites irresponsible and unaccountable cheap shots. You will want to discuss and consider this issue before administering any survey.

Disaggregation. When you are reporting on your data, you may wish to total and analyze responses based on the subpopulations from which they were derived. For example, did the opinions of the girls in the classes differ from the opinions of the boys? Did the outlook of teachers who had been in the building for more than ten years differ from that of new teachers? Did parents with higher levels of education perceive our school more or less favorably than parents with less formal education? If you decide that you want to draw inferences like these from your data (survey and interview data are particularly good for this purpose), you will also need to obtain appropriate demographic data through your survey or interview. Be careful that your requests for demographic information don't compromise any assurances of anonymity. For example, if you ask teachers in a small school to tell you their gender, number of years in the school, and teaching assignment, they may rightly believe that anonymity is impossible.

Reporting back. As mentioned earlier, people generally are flattered to have their opinions solicited and will be generous with their time; they are justified, however, in wanting something in return. What they usually want is feedback. At the time of your survey or interview, you need to be prepared to tell your subjects how you intend to report back any results obtained. If respondents believe you are sitting on unflattering data, your future credibility will be irrevocably damaged.

Capturing the Data. Verbatim responses provide one of the richest sources of information you will find. When a research report quotes the responses of individuals, the report becomes the equivalent of a geography textbook filled with maps, photos, and colorful illustrations. To ensure that you do have verbatim quotes, it is best to tape-record interviews (always with the permission of the person you're interviewing). Tape-recording allows you, the interviewer, to listen actively and give your subject both eye contact and your undivided attention. It also allows you to have a complete and accurate record of the discussion. If tape-recording is impossible, you may want to try using two interviewers; one person can be the listener while the other tries to take verbatim notes.

Triangulation

Earlier in this chapter, we discussed the importance of validity and reliability. Ensuring that research findings are of high quality is as important an issue for the action researcher as for anyone doing scientific inquiry, for conducting research is a time-consuming activity, and you don't want to waste your time collecting unreliable data. Unreliable data will cause you to lose confidence in your results and will cause others to question the validity of your conclusions. Remember that the purpose of collaborative action research is to help you *take action* to improve your school or classroom. If the changes you undertake are based on ill-formed ideas that are the result of invalid and unreliable data, they will probably fail. And the ultimate result will be students who don't perform as well as they could and teachers who feel less competent. Sound research, on the other hand, usually leads to equally sound recommendations for change that will improve student performance and enhance teachers' professional self-esteem.

The quality issue raises a perplexing question for action researchers. Short of investing the time and energy required to become experts in research methodology and instrument development, how can teacher-researchers be sure that their data collection methods are reliable? Realistically, there is no sure solution here, but paying attention to a technique called triangulation will go a long way toward improving the quality of your findings. Simply put, triangulation involves collecting multiple sources of data for every phenomenon or issue being studied.

In our work with collaborative action researchers, we have operationally defined triangulation as using at least three independent windows on whatever phenomenon is being studied. How does this help ensure quality? Let's look at an analogy. Imagine a 3rd grade science lesson on the subject of "observation." The teacher asks Mary to look through the front panel of the classroom terrarium and list or draw everything she sees. Mary, being a diligent student, writes up a thorough list. She's just about to go back to her seat when the teacher asks her to take a look through the side panel of the terrarium. Mary does, and immediately sees several plants and animals that had been obscured from view in the front panel by rocks and shrubs. By using this second "window" on the phenomenon (the terrarium), Mary now has a more complete picture.

Although Mary feels that her work is now done, the teacher makes one last request. She asks Mary to peer through the top of the terrarium to see if there is anything else she has missed. Mary adds to her list and then sits down. Although Mary may still have failed to observe something of importance, her three windows reveal a far more comprehensive picture than any one window alone could have.

Let's look at another example of triangulation, this one involving an investigation of classroom practice. Say I wanted to investigate my use of cooperative learning structures in my classroom. I might choose to have a colleague observe my class, I might evaluate my own performance as captured on videotape, and I might have another colleague interview my students. If all three windows on my cooperative learning lesson end up showing the same picture, then that picture is likely a valid portrait of my teaching. But suppose that I rated my instruction as inspiring, while my colleague and my students saw it in quite a different light. That discrepancy (a potential source for further inquiry) would have been lost had I used a single measure.

I recall that one school we worked with was investigating the causes of student alienation. The action researchers surveyed students, parents, and teachers. On the issue of staff caring the teachers gave themselves high marks (an average of 9 on a 10-point scale), while students and parents viewed teachers as aloof and cold. More particularly, the less successful students felt strongly that their teachers didn't care about them. Although this discordant information was painful for the teachers to consider, it became the inspiration for much valuable work. Teachers became intensely interested in finding out exactly what they were doing that caused students and parents to perceive them this way. The response to this one item on the survey was a primary force behind the introduction of a teacher advisory program in the school.

In summary, triangulation provides these benefits:

• It compensates for the imperfections of data-gathering instruments.

• When multiple measures yield the same results, it can increase confidence in the results.

• When multiple measures fail to yield the same results, it can raise important follow-up questions.

Making a Data-Collection Plan

Using a matrix like the one in Figure 4.4, you can develop a complete data-collection plan for your project. First, list each of the research questions that surfaced in the problem formulation process. Then for each question, determine at least three independent windows for collecting data on the question being investigated.

Figure 4.4
Data Collection Plan

Research Questions	Data Source #1	Data Source #2	Data Source #3

The Role of the Critical Friend

Collecting data is a time-consuming activity. In fact, it is the single most labor-intensive part of the collaborative action research process. Nothing can be more frustrating than to complete your data collection and find that you didn't ask the right questions or observe the right phenomena or gather the right information from the files. An excellent way to guard against incomplete or short-sighted data collection is to follow the old axiom "two heads are better than one." And we would add that three heads are better than two. One of the advantages of working collaboratively in action research teams is that team members can analyze and critique one another's data collection plans, all the while surfacing additional questions and issues for consideration. Many projects also benefit from the introduction of a third party, a "critical friend."

A critical friend is just what the name implies. A person who has your interests at heart when she gives you constructive criticism. This person's outside vantage point allows her to see your weaknesses better than you can, but because this person is a friend, she's likely to be critical of your weaknesses in a positive way. She is critiquing you because she cares about you. You probably have many friends you could ask to play the role of critical friend: colleagues from other buildings, professors, educational consultants, leaders from educational organizations (groups like ASCD, NCTM, NCTE, etc.), administrators, supervisors, and specialists. What makes for a good critical friend, besides the typical qualities of friendship, is expertise concerning the tasks at hand. When working on data collection, the expertise needed is often in the area of research methodology or instrument development. Expertise concerning the particular phenomenon you are studying might not be as important at this stage (though if you were consulting a critical friend at the problem formulation stage, content knowledge might be very helpful). In fact, a certain degree of naivete about the phenomenon under study often can prove helpful for a critical friend.

When you bring in a critical friend, you must be careful to avoid what my colleague Peter Holly calls the consultancy trap. This trap is set when a team invites a third party in to help and subtly defers to this person's superior expertise, letting him take over the direction of the project. Before they know it, the team members find that they are subordinates in their own research efforts. To avoid the consultancy trap, we at Project LEARN have developed a set of guidelines that we expect our cadre of critical friends to adhere to. You may want to share this list with anyone your team plans to ask to be a critical friend:

• The critical friend will be chosen based on the needs and desires of the project participants.

• The critical friend will not have any stake in the problem being addressed or in the outcome of the project unless such ownership is granted by the participants.

• The critical friend is a positive friend whose primary agenda is to assist in moving the project toward success.

• The critical friend may have a personal agenda complementary to the project agenda. The critical friend will share with the participants his or her motives or intents at the time of the first interaction.

• The critical friend is a visitor and participates only at the continued invitation of the project participants.

• The critical friend will respond and act honestly at every juncture.

• It is the obligation of the critical friend to declare any conflict of interest or conflict of values with the project focus or methods.

• The critical friend will assume that the project's interactions, work, and findings are confidential unless the project directs otherwise.

• The participants are expected to assist the critical friend by fully informing them of all agendas prior to each consultation.

5
Data Analysis

YOUR TEAM NOW HAS BUSHEL BASKETS OF INTERVIEW TRANSCRIPTS, completed surveys, summaries of test results, observation checklists, and the like. But what does all this data tell us? To find out, we have to analyze the data. Data analysis can be most simply described as a process of sifting, sorting, discarding, and cataloguing in an attempt to answer two basic questions: (1) What are the important themes in this data? and (2) How much data support each of these themes? The process of data analysis involves two sequential stages.

Identifying Themes

This first stage takes advantage of our unique human ability to gain insight through intuition. The team meets in a comfortable atmosphere and in round-robin fashion reads through all the assembled data, sifting through it to try to get a clear view of the big picture. If there is a large amount of data, the team may want to have each person read only a portion of the whole and report back to the rest of the team. The team then identifies themes, issues, or factors that seem to be emerging from the data. These are generally of two types: (a) items that come up repeatedly or (b) idiosyncratic items that seem particularly noteworthy.

This initial review of the data is aimed at developing fortuitous insights. It allows the researchers to react intuitively to the data, to voice their gut reactions. Sometimes this process is called "skimming."

"Interrogating" the Data

Once the skimming process has been completed, the team should begin to use a scientific codification process to "interrogate" the data. Whereas the skimming process helped the team come to grips with what they "thought" or "felt" was in the data, this second stage helps the team transform themselves into Perry Masons who are on a mission to determine whether the evidence truly supports their theories.

Using a Matrix

The interrogation process can be accomplished by drawing up a matrix for data sorting on 8 1/2″ by 11″ sheets or on 6′ or 9′ sheets of paper on the wall of the faculty room. Across the top of the paper are written each of the themes or categories that emerged during the skimming stage. For example, if you were studying the factors associated with student success at your school, you might have sensed that the following themes were significant or prevalent in your data: past success in school, parent involvement, relationships with teachers, and relationships with peers. Those items would be listed on the top of the paper, as illustrated in Figure 5.1 on the next page.

On the vertical axis is placed either individual sources of data (surveys, interviews, test scores, and so on) or, if only one data source was used, data from individual respondents. As the team members read through the raw data, they look for supporting data for each of the themes in the matrix. When they discover a piece of data pertaining to a theme, they write it in the appropriate space on the matrix. (Note: New themes almost always emerge during this phase. When they do, they are simply added as new boxes on the matrix.) For example, when we are reviewing data from survey or interview transcripts, we might find comments like this: "Its very important to my parents that I do well in school. My father thinks that an education is the only way out of this neighborhood." "My parents don't care about my grades. They said once I'm sixteen, if I can find a job, I can drop out." These comments would be placed under the category of Interviews/Parent Involvement, as shown in Figure 5.2 on page 51.

Figure 5.1
Data Matrix

	Previous Experience	Parent Involvement	Relationships with Teachers
Surveys			
Interviews			
Archival Evidence			

Figure 5.2
Data Matrix

	Previous Experience	Parent Involvement	Relationships with Teachers
Surveys			
Interviews		"It's very important to my parents that I do well in school. My father thinks that an education is the only way out of this neighborhood." (Subject 3) "My parents don't care about my grades. They said once I'm sixteen, if I can find a job, I can drop out." (Subject 7)	"I work hard for the teachers who show an interest in me. If a teacher talks to me in the halls and seems to recognize that I'm a human being, I'm willing to work for them. The others can go to hell as far as I'm concerned!" (Subject 6) "When teachers relate the work to my life, I'm interested. If I can't see how it applies to my life, I'm bored." (Subject 9)
Archival Evidence	Eighty-five percent of the students who had GPAs of 3.5 or above in junior high school had GPAs of 3.5 or above in high school. Ninety-one percent of the students who had received remedial services in elementary school also received them in high school.		

Quotes like the following would be placed under the category of Interviews/Relationships with Teachers: "I work hard for the teachers who show an interest in me. If a teacher talks to me in the halls and seems to recognize that I'm a human being, I'm willing to work for them. The others can go to hell as far as I'm concerned!" "When teachers relate the work to my life, I'm interested. If I can't see how it applies to my life, I'm bored."

Finally, statistics like the following would be written under the category of Archival Evidence/Previous Experiences: "Eighty-five percent of the students with 3.5 GPAs or above in junior high had 3.5 or above in high school." "Ninety-one percent of the students receiving remedial services in elementary school were receiving them in high school."

Once this process has been completed, the team will have a visual representation of their data that is similar to stacking all the books in the school library by category so a casual observer can see if the stacks of biographies are higher or lower than the mysteries or the reference books.

Remember, going into data analysis, we had two questions: (1) What are the important themes in this data? and (2) How much data support each of these themes? To answer these questions, we first look at the matrix to see which themes have the most supporting data. Then we summarize the data. For instance, if students repeatedly mentioned issues regarding their teachers, yet never mentioned their peers, then it would be fair to summarize the data in a statement worded along these lines: "The students in our school mentioned teacher relationships as a factor in their performance five times more frequently than they mentioned issues with peers, parents, or administrators."

Themes that do not have the support of an abundance of data may still seem significant to the team because of the specific nature of the supporting data. The team can word their data summary to reflect their concern, as in this example: "While only seven students mentioned difficulty in establishing friendships, that amounted to over half of the transfer students we interviewed."

Coding Surveys and Transcripts

When action researchers have to analyze many journal entries, interview transcripts, or surveys containing open-ended questions, they often will use a coding process to organize the data. The basic steps of the coding process are as follows:

1. Create bins for each category of data (these bins are analogous to the cells on the data analysis matrix). Bin categories may emerge from the skimming stage or from the creation of the graphic representation in the earlier problem formulation stage.

2. Assign a color code to each bin. For example, parent issues could be pink, teacher issues blue, and peer issues yellow.

3. Carefully read through the data, highlighting with an appropriately colored marker the sentences, paragraphs, or phrases belonging in each bin. Note that some data could be placed in more than one bin.

4. Group statements of one color together in a single document. If you have done your highlighting on paper lists that have not been transferred to a computer file, you'll have to retype the lists. If you had typed your data on a computer file, you may be able to use the "sort" function to expedite this process.

5. Before gathering statements of the same color, tag each with the source of the data, because once the bins have been sorted, it will be difficult to retrace the origin of the data.

6. Summarize the data as appropriate—for instance, with statistics or key examples as shown in the "Archival Evidence" section of the data matrix shown in Figure 5.2.

Forming New Conclusions

Action research has been described as peeling away layers of an onion. Removing one layer usually reveals another layer that prompts further examination. For example, finding out that cooperative learning has been successful for *most* students might cause us to ask what makes it unsuccessful for others. And finding out that 90 percent of students who perform poorly in junior high school also perform poorly in high school might prompt us to want to know what changed things for the 10 percent of low-achievers who ultimately turned it around.

This peeling away of layers can help you move toward more complete understanding of the specific educational phenomena you are studying. In fact, it is at the end of the data analysis process that the team often comes to new conclusions about the phenomena under study. After summarizing the data, the team returns to the graphic representation created during the problem formulation phase. The graphic initially served to illustrate your theoretical understandings, such as they were at that point. Now that you have more data and presumably know far more about the issue under study, you can review your graphic representation:

• You can make solid some of the dotted lines indicating presumed relationships, now that you know better whether those relationships do, in fact, exist.

• You can add factors and variables to your original conceptual theory.

• You can delete any presumptions that are no longer valid.

In our first year with Project LEARN, we had a team from an elementary school that chose to investigate the factors influencing the low performance of students in their school. Their graphic representation showed that the faculty (and the action research team) believed that the socioeconomic status of their school was a major factor in the low performance of their students on standardized tests. In fact, the teachers contended that the "apartment kids" (those whose families lived in the low-income housing units in the area) were bringing the aggregate scores down. The data they gathered, however, showed that the apartment kids were outscoring the kids who lived in single-family housing. The teachers began looking elsewhere for explanations and found them in their teaching practices. As a result, teaching strategies have changed and student performance has improved.

Another relevant example comes from elementary school teachers who were investigating why their school's spelling program wasn't very successful. As part of the data collection, they surveyed parents. The teachers were surprised and a bit upset to find that parents held extremely negative views of the school's new "language experience" approach to spelling. Apparently, the parents had other ideas on how spelling ought to be taught. That discovery radically changed the teachers' focus for improvement. They realized their problem was most likely not the students, as they had originally presumed, or the program itself, as parents had suggested; instead, the problem was almost certainly a lack of communication and cooperation between the school and parents. As a result, the teachers committed themselves to an initiative inviting parents to be partners in the teaching of spelling. Figure 5.3 shows the staff's graphic representation before their data collection, and Figure 5.4 shows the graphic representation after their data analysis.

Figure 5.3
Graphic Representation of Problem Before Data Collection

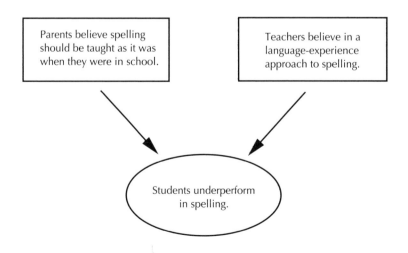

Figure 5.4
Graphic Representation of Problem After Data Analysis

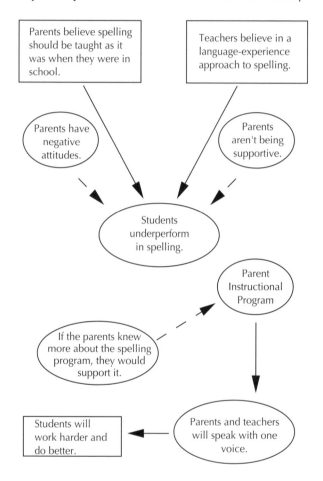

If our only interest in collaborative action research were to gain knowledge for its own sake, our work would be finished when we concluded our data analysis. Because our goals are greater, however, it is vitally important to tend to the next stages in the process: reporting and action planning. Chapters 6 and 7 discuss these two critical components of collaborative action research.

6
Reporting Results

THE REPORTING OF RESEARCH IS NOT OFTEN DISCUSSED IN ACTION research circles. Because collaborative action research is conducted primarily for the benefit of the teacher-researchers involved, consideration of wider audiences is, unfortunately, generally thought to be superfluous or irrelevant. When we consider the many purposes for pursuing collaborative action research (discussed in Chapter 1), however, the importance of reporting becomes clear.

The Purposes of Collaborative Action Research

To Break the Isolation

In our early training programs, if participants wanted to receive academic credit they were required to formally present their findings in a forum of their choice—for instance, at a faculty meeting, a district meeting, or a state or national conference. It was troubling and surprising to note that participants were generally relieved to find out they could satisfy this requirement by reporting before strangers at a large conference rather than by talking to the colleagues they worked with every day. This reaction helped us realize that breaking the code of silence and making legitimate the regular discussion of classroom practice would be a major side benefit of creating an action research reporting program.

To Contribute to the Knowledge Base

The issues that have been troubling teachers in your department or school are probably not unique. In all likelihood, other teachers are concerned about similar teaching and learning issues and would welcome the opportunity to read or hear about your insights and revelations, your decisions and puzzlements. For some reason, many teachers believe that others won't be interested in what they have to offer. I've even heard some teachers introduce themselves at parties with the three-word title "Just A Teacher." Unless and until we find ways to include classroom teachers in the serious discourse about teaching and learning, teachers will continue to be forced to implement research based on questions hatched in laboratories, far from the realities of the public school classroom.

To Gain a Voice in Quality Control

I vividly remember an experience from an English department where I taught. My colleagues were an outstanding group of writing teachers who were working at the cutting edge of the "writing process" movement. Two years in a row, the superintendent of schools came by after the standardized test scores had arrived to ask us what was going wrong. Our scores were reflecting something far from excellence. I remember how we argued that our students' actual writing would reflect a far different picture. We assured the superintendent that an analysis of students' work before and after the implementation of the writing process and comparisons of their work with that of students from other schools would show our students to be quite proficient. He appeared to be unpersuaded, but was willing to listen. Unfortunately, we never presented any data (I still believe if we had, he would have been impressed). The following year, the curriculum office began asserting itself and forcing its biases into our writing curriculum. Our department had been given a chance to participate in quality control, but by not collecting and sharing data, we lost an important political battle.

Reporting on research is essential not only for these above purposes, but for fostering a school culture that promotes learning for all.

The Structure of an Action Research Report

One of the nice things about reporting action research is the freedom you have in choosing how to present what you have learned. The professional research community has developed rules and conventions regarding scientific presentation (see, for example, the *Publication Manual of the American Psychological Association*) that, while enforcing some degree of rigor through standardization, may also stifle enthusiasm and creativity, both of which are hallmarks of collaborative action research. Since action research reports are developed by and for practitioners, the most important consideration should be to choose a method that will tell the story accurately and effectively. Many collaborative action research reports contain mixtures of media, including (but not limited to) videotapes, photographs, charts and figures, written narratives, audiotapes, and oral presentations. Whatever the method of presentation, the format of a successful report generally follows this outline:

- Introduction
- A description of the research process
- An analysis of the data
- An action plan

Each section answers important questions for your audience, and considering them together allows other educators to determine if your findings are relevant to their local circumstances.

Introduction

At the beginning of your report, you want to tell the audience about the site where the research was conducted, the focus of the research, and any pertinent characteristics of the staff and students. Fully explaining the context is extremely important. As mentioned earlier, with action research we aren't very concerned about generalizability; we are conducting the research primarily for ourselves. The purpose of the report is simply to invite our colleagues to look over our shoulders as we work. It will ultimately be up to them to determine if our findings are applicable to their setting. An introduction to an action research report might read something like this:

This study was conducted by four members of the 5th grade team at Riverwalk Elementary School, one of thirty-seven schools in the River City School District. We are a 500-student, K–6 magnet school with students who are admitted on a first-come, first-served basis; however, our student body is required to mirror the racial composition of the city (35 percent white, 25 percent African-American, 25 percent Hispanic, 10 percent Asian). We were concerned about the comparatively low performance of our students on measures of reading comprehension, so we began an investigation of the relationship between improved comprehension and both recreational reading (free reading and library time) and classroom assignments.

A Description of the Research Process

In the second section of the report, you want to describe the research process(es) you engaged in. Whereas the introduction answered the question "Who are you and what were you studying?" this section answers the question "What did you do?" This section should clearly and concisely explain the research procedures you followed. It might sound something like this:

We pretested all of the children on the STRC (Sagor Test of Reading Comprehension) at the end of September. During the months of October and November, all the teachers and students kept logs of all reading assigned and accomplished in and outside class. A post-test was administered the first week of December. In addition, we interviewed twenty-five randomly chosen students and conducted separate telephone interviews with their parents to determine their outside-of-school reading habits, preferences, and attitudes toward school. Each member of the research team visited each of the five 5th grade classrooms at least once during reading time to observe the instructional strategies being used. We then contrasted the data on the reading experiences of students who showed dramatic growth, moderate growth, and no growth to see if any trends or patterns were evident.

An Analysis of the Data

At this point, your audience should be clear about who you are, what you were interested in, and what you did. Whether their school is just like yours or vastly different is a matter they can extrapolate from your description of context. This third section of the report should tell the audience what you found out. The data section of action research reports is usually more interesting than its counterpart in scientific reports because action researchers usually feel free to use more vivid means of illustration. In addition to statistics, charts, and graphs, I've seen examples of student work (from portfolios), heard segments of interviews on audiotape, and seen both videotaped portions of lessons and testimonials from teachers and students.

An Action Plan

At this stage, you should be thinking of your report as a discussion between two colleagues. As I'm listening to what your team has to say, I have received a clear picture of what your classrooms are like, the issues that concerned you, what you looked at, and what you learned. Now I want to know what you're going to do as a result. When doing an oral presentation of your research, this section of your presentation should be given the most time on the agenda. As teachers, we are all action-oriented professionals. Your analyses of the data will already have given you ideas for next steps, and any colleagues who are listening to your report will be quite interested in hearing what meaning you derived from your findings. And they will probably want to share ideas of their own about the implications of your study. I have observed hundreds of reports of collaborative action research projects, and never have I ceased to be impressed by the quality of the discussions concerning the implications of the studies.

Venues for Reporting

There are many audiences for your work, just as there are many purposes for presenting what you have learned. Some audiences and purposes call for formal presentations, while others are clearly more ad hoc and informal. Among the potential audiences are: policymakers, school boards, parent groups, community groups, state agencies, professional associations, university classes, conference sessions, association journals or bulletins, Phi Delta Kappa meetings, colleagues, department or grade level meetings, faculty meetings, and district committees.

Although each of these audiences is important, the methods for addressing them will be different. Earlier in the book, I argued that an important purpose of collaborative action research is to bring about a cultural transformation of the school. That cultural transformation will occur only when we institutionalize opportunities for sharing with colleagues. I have seen a number of successful models for achieving this end.

The Rotating Faculty Meeting

Every month, one faculty meeting is held in a different classroom with the entire agenda devoted to sharing what has been learned through reflective practice. Faculties who spend at least ten meetings a year putting colleagues front and center, sharing what they've learned about teaching and learning via systematic analysis of practice, become faculties who have institutionalized the norms of experimentation and collegiality.

The District Conference

An inservice day is used for a conference involving district educators, although often educators from surrounding communities are invited to attend. On the surface, the format looks like a traditional education conference, but each session is presented by district educators who share what they have learned in their own local studies. When institutionalized as annual events, such programs drive home the point that the knowledge needed to inform practice can be derived locally. It sends to district teachers the powerful message that they are in the driver's seat, rather than just being taken along for the ride.

The District Journal

The district can publish a quarterly journal containing reports of action research (as well as educational commentaries) from local teachers. In districts where this strategy has been institutionalized, the journal begins to take on the aura of a publication like *Educational Leadership*.

Each issue might have a theme for which articles are solicited and also feature general submissions (action research reports of an idiosyncratic nature, papers prepared for college classes, and the like) and even an occasional piece of creative writing or artwork done by a staff member. Seeing our work in print can give us a special kind of empowerment. Ideas come alive when they can be discussed and debated by a wider audience. Teachers who have published their work report seeing their contributions as having increased significance.

The Regional Action Research Conference

For several years now, Project LEARN and the Puget Sound Consortium (a collaborative project of the University of Washington and local area districts) have co-hosted an annual International Symposium on Action Research. The conference is held each April at a large convention hotel in one of the major Northwest cities. It is structured to provide a vehicle for action researchers to make public their work. Typically, more than 100 teacher-researchers present their studies to several hundred attending teachers who are eager to learn what their colleagues have been doing.

A Final Note on Reporting

The reporting of research serves several critical as well as practical purposes. It disseminates important findings. It advances our practice. And it gives us fresh insights by requiring us to organize our material for presentation. Just as important, though are the symbolic purposes. By taking the time to report our findings, we remind ourselves and tell others that our work is important and worthy of consideration. In keeping with that symbolic role, it is important that the entire set-up of the presentation be of a caliber and quality befitting to professional endeavors. Refreshments should be served at faculty meetings, conferences should be held in first-class hotels, and journals should be typeset on high-quality paper. Administrators and policymakers need to realize that the relatively minor additional cost of treating practicing educators as they would prestigious consultants and scientists is not a frivolous expenditure, but a visible confirmation of the importance of these professionals to the educational system.

7
Putting the Action
Into Action Research

EVEN IF YOU FOLLOWED ALL THE STEPS OUTLINED IN THIS BOOK UP TO this point, you wouldn't be finished with the action research process, because action research is all about taking action based on systematically collected data. Once you have your data, it's time to proceed with action. Taking action is not always easy, however.

In Chapter 2, I suggested that action research should be conducted within one's sphere of influence. Spheres of influence, however, usually fall along a continuum. On one extreme are issues controlled by the classroom teacher—for example, how to manage students, organize lessons, or administer day-to-day tests. On the other extreme are matters that require a collaborative effort to be fully successful. These two different contexts make all the difference in planning how to take action.

Action planning is primarily a matter of will for action researchers who are undertaking changes bounded only by the walls of their own classrooms. It is important for these teachers to revisit their graphic representation and be sure that their conceptual base and their data support the implementation of a new initiative. Then, being mindful of time constraints, they should simply plunge in and put their plan into practice.

The task is a little trickier for action researchers who find they need support and collaboration to successfully take action. The difficulty is that collaborative change inevitably involves changing the behavior of people who have not been involved in the research effort. Many people have observed that schools are slow to change. Why is that? Is it because educators are conservative by nature? Are we lazy? Do we not have students' best interests at heart? The answer is "no" on all three counts. In fact, I suspect the reason schools are so slow to change is that teachers are, for the most part, already doing what they believe is best for their students.

Cognitive dissonance theory tells us that to reduce stress, human beings strive for congruence between their behavior and beliefs (Festinger 1957); therefore, teachers would have to be psychologically unbalanced to deliberately not make changes they believed would benefit students. The fact is that many teachers have good reason to interpret colleagues' or administrators' calls for change as requests to abandon what's best for their students and instead conduct irresponsible experiments on them. You can hardly fault any teacher for resisting such requests.

Another reason many schools are slow to change is that they already have made many deliberate compromises to establish their current way of doing things. The great American psychologist Kurt Lewin (who is also the father of action research) explains the phenomenon at work here as a "force field" (see Figure 7.1 on p. 68); that is, the current way of doing things is the point at which the forces for change (pressures to innovate, experiment, etc.) are equally matched by the forces against change. Schools are held in place, or frozen, by these opposing forces. Thus, the collaborative action research team must concentrate on weakening, or unfreezing, the force of those who are against change. Although this task may at first seem quite formidable, it will not seem so for long if you enter the discussion armed with a powerful weapon: your data.

Using Data to Overcome Biases

Most debates in schools are debates over biases. Whether we are debating tracking, whole language, or approaches to discipline, the lines that separate faculty factions are usually beliefs and assumptions. The teachers on one side argue that they believe there is a better way. They read some research about it, or they believe it's the wave of the future. Teachers on the other side counter with,

Figure 7.1
The Force-Field Phenomenon

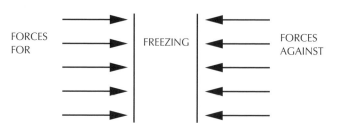

"We've seen it all before. Besides, you can find research to support any position." A battle ensues, and change generally doesn't occur. Even worse, the reformers often leave the fray fatigued and disillusioned, thinking that change is impossible. Tragically, many fine teachers ultimately decide to leave the profession because experience has convinced them that innovation and change won't ever occur. What we need to realize is that the primary reason people don't change their opinion in these debates is that no evidence is offered to make them even begin to question their beliefs (i.e., their biases). And if there is no good reason to question their beliefs, which are congruent with their behavior, why go through the stress of change?

Data that bring our previous behavior into question create cognitive dissonance; in other words, evidence indicating that our beliefs may not be correct can cause us to reconsider those beliefs. Compelling data are just the agent that action researchers need to enable the school or district to move laterally, as illustrated in Figure 7.2.

Now let's look at four basic strategies for managing dissonance and changing the status quo.

Figure 7.2
The Effect of Compelling Data on the Force Field

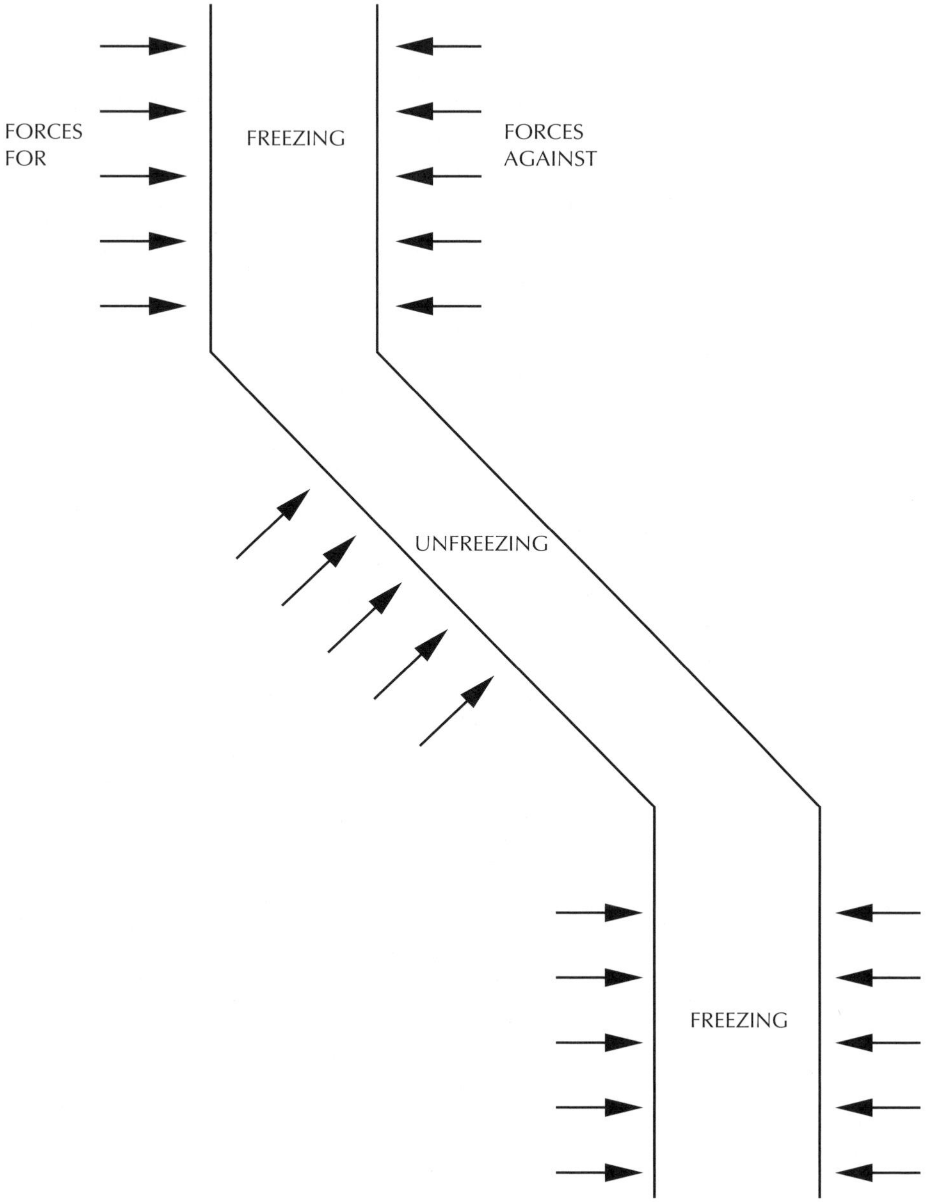

FORCES
FOR

FREEZING

FORCES
AGAINST

UNFREEZING

FREEZING

Strategy 1: Simply Present The Data.

Sometimes unembellished data alone can convince people of the need for change. For instance, perhaps you are teaching mathematics in a high school on the West coast with many low-income students and a faculty that has held low expectations for student achievement. Your colleagues believe that children living in poverty shouldn't be expected to do college prep mathematics. You may be able to convince them otherwise simply by showing the film *Stand and Deliver*, or reading excerpts from Jay Mathews' book *Escalante: The Best Teacher in America*, or reviewing the data on the math program created by Jaime Escalante at Garfield High School. The data may be so compelling that your colleagues will immediately set about trying to change their teaching strategies and expectations.

Strategy 2: Establish a Pilot Program.

Schools that encourage collaborative action research are places that have usually legitimized entrepreneurial initiatives. For this reason, if the results of your collaborative action research project point to promising school reforms, yet many of your colleagues remain unconvinced, you may want to get permission to conduct a pilot project. In developing a pilot, it is important to make every effort to have the pilot group resemble the school as a whole in terms of students' past performance, ethnicity, dollars per pupil, time allocated, and so on. The implementation of the pilot program should include a strong "research of action" (evaluation) data collection plan.

One advantage of this approach is that naysayers won't be able to disrupt your program. You will be moving ahead with those people who want to participate. And if your pilot works and your action research data support what you have claimed, then the people who initially resisted will have little choice but to accept the value of your program. The discussion on change can then move from a debate over biases to a debate over data.

Strategy 3: Establish Competing Pilot Programs

In a school that has institutionalized the ethic of action research and has made pilot programs an accepted form of experimentation, collaborative action research can provide a wonderful mechanism for resolving or focusing debate. Imagine a school where the faculty is divided on reading practices. One contingent is committed to using a basal reader and skills-based instruction. Another contingent is committed to whole-language instruction. If the two groups debate, the argument could run well into the night and, in all likelihood, nothing would be resolved. Instead, why not run two concurrent collaborative action research projects?

The first step would be to have both groups agree on outcome criteria for successful reading performance. Then, one group goes ahead and does its best teaching of whole language, all the while collecting data on the results using the agreed-upon criteria. Meanwhile the other group uses its basal readers and proceeds with skill-based instruction, also collecting data as they go. What are the possible outcomes?

• The basal group could end up demonstrating that its approach was superior. If that occurred, the whole-language group would be expected to support what's best for the kids.

• The whole-language approach could show itself to be superior, and then the basal supporters would be expected to line up behind the whole-language program.

• Finally, the worst-case scenario could happen: there could be no appreciable difference between the groups. Such a result would prove that perhaps there is no definitive answer to this question (yet), and both approaches could (and maybe should) continue side by side.

Regardless, of the outcome of the experiment, the ensuing debate would be over data, not biases, thus reinforcing an atmosphere of mutual professional respect.

In one high-performing middle school where we worked, the teachers were locked in a debate over tracking. Pilot programs were put in place and data were collected. The result? No significant differences were found between the tracked and untracked groups. But an interesting thing happened. This school had been tracked for more than twenty-five years with much support from the senior faculty. All the teachers in this school, young and old, had great respect for one another. When the data didn't really support one approach over the other, the senior faculty, who had been defending the tracking system for years, relented and in essence said, "We had our chance for twenty-five years. Now we're willing give the other approach a try." Although a response of this nature is not to be expected in every school, it is an example of what can happen in a school that has a culture of professional and collegial respect.

Strategy 4: Use the Research as Educational Specifications

In this strategy, the collaborative action research team works as a research arm of the faculty (or of a smaller unit such as a department or a grade level) in a joint effort toward school improvement. This is a four-step strategy:

a. Define the problem. Using techniques like the ones discussed in Chapter 3 or other decision-making strategies, the entire faculty or work group (for example, a department, a grade level, or a districtwide committee) could identify a school improvement issue that is of general concern.

b. Understand the problem. A collaborative action research team is then asked to take over and conduct a study of the issue identified by the work group. The goal of the study is to develop as full an understanding as possible about how this issue is being played out in the local context.

c. Brainstorm/seek out action alternatives. Once the action research team has presented this report on the issue, the larger faculty work group is asked to develop a list of possible approaches for solving the problem, usually by brainstorming as many ideas as possible. Another method for surfacing alternative strategies is to solicit approaches used in other schools. The result should be a comprehensive list of proposals for approaching the issue at hand.

d. Proof the proposals. The work group then prepares a force-field analysis chart like the one in Figure 7.3 for each of the action alternatives. Often these charts are prepared on sheets of paper big enough to fill a classroom wall. At the top of each sheet, the proposal is summarized. Time is provided to have each proposal explained fully enough for everyone to understand what is being proposed. The key word here is *explained* not *discussed*. Debate should not occur at this point; only clarifying questions are considered to be in order.

Figure 7.3
Force-Field Analysis Chart

Action alternative # _____

Description of action alternative: _____

_____

_____

_____

Forces For	Forces Against

Then data from the action research study are used to fill in the charts. Data that point to a reason why a proposal is likely to succeed are listed as "forces for." Data that imply a problem with the proposal are listed as "forces against." After all the charts have been filled in, the group should be able to clearly see which proposals have the most research evidence supporting them and which do not.

Occasionally, it becomes apparent that additional research is needed, and the action research team can take on the responsibility to collect that data. Once the faculty or the work group (or both) are satisfied that they have enough data to make a decision, they can proceed to endorse one of the action alternatives—the one with the most research support, we would hope.

* * *

Which approach to action planning is right for you or your team can be determined only by analyzing the culture of your school. Ultimately, the change process you use will need to be tailored to fit the local context.

8
A Final Word

No One Way _____

NO TWO APPROACHES TO ACTION RESEARCH ARE EXACTLY ALIKE.
The perspective in this book may be at odds with the views
of others working in this field. Some authors discuss action
research primarily as a teacher development strategy.
Others describe it as a special mode of discourse. And still
others argue that it is an act of political liberation. Each of
these approaches has merit, and I believe no one approach
is incompatible with another. In the interests of time and
space, however, I chose to focus on the collaborative
process of school-based research. I have discussed action
research primarily as a school development strategy, since
this approach has such promise for changing the
professional culture of the school. The exclusion of the
other approaches to action research should not be
interpreted as an oversight or a denigration of the merits
of alternative perspectives.

A Model, Not a Prescription _____

I have outlined a set of procedures that collaborative
action researchers might want to consider when conducting
studies of their own practice. These suggestions were
offered with some trepidation. Collaborative action
research is a process that respects teachers'
professionalism, intelligence, and decision-making abilities.
At its core, the process values empowerment, initiative, and
experimentation. We cannot hold those values and then be
authoritative, orthodox, or prescriptive about methodology.
For that reason, the strategies offered in this book are to be

taken as starting points, and action research teams should feel free to modify strategies if, on reflection, alternative approaches seem to better fit their local context.

Professional researchers may well find my descriptions of research concepts too abbreviated and overly simplistic for their taste. Likewise, teachers may see some of the steps of the research process as far too cumbersome. Both criticisms may be correct; however, the strategies suggested are the result of more than mere conjecture. They have worked for dozens of action research teams that I have worked with. Thus, it is with full cognizance of the criticisms that might be raised that I have offered these strategies for your consideration.

A Perhaps Glaring Omission

Nowhere in this book have I talked about the use of grounded theory. It could appear as though I am suggesting that all knowledge must be empirically discerned by the teacher-researchers themselves. This would be wrong, and I hope the reader doesn't assume that action researchers should disregard or discredit our preexisting knowledge bases. Nor would I want to imply that there is no merit in consulting the literature prior to embarking on a study. The value of conducting a formal review of the literature before conducting original research is an efficiency that scientists have historically found both helpful and productive. It is no less valuable for action researchers.

I would encourage anyone interested in doing good research to review the literature immediately after engaging in the problem formulation activities suggested in Chapter 3. The reason for omitting a review of the research from the five-step process presented in this text is that for many first-time action researchers, a trip to the library is a turn-off. After all, as full-time teachers they are primarily interested in matters of practice, not research. A day off from the classroom to peruse journals doesn't, on the surface, seem like a worthwhile investment of time. For that reason, we have elected to go with the first-timer's natural bias for action. We give them an opportunity to get their hands dirty in collecting data, being informed initially by only their craft knowledge, prior education, and reflective discussions. Experience has shown us that after one successful research project, collaborative action researchers will choose to consult the knowledge base in a more formal fashion to inform their future studies.

The premise of action research is that best practice continues to evolve and differs from context to context. This is also the case with the practice of collaborative action research. Just as we want our teaching to be of the highest quality, we should want no less of our research. As you use the collaborative action research process, you will be experimenting and discovering new and better methods of practice. That is as it should be. It is my sincere hope that this book has provided you with a helpful starting point. Have a great journey!

References and Resources

Carr, W., and S. Kemmis. *Becoming Critical: Education Knowledge and Action Research.* London: Falmer Press.

Clift, R.T., W.R. Houston, and M.C. Pugach. (1990). *Encouraging Reflective Practice in Education.* New York: Teachers College Press.

Corey, S.M. (1953). *Action Research to Improve School Practices.* New York: Teachers College Press.

Festinger, L. (1957). *A Theory of Cognitive Dissonance.* Stanford, Calif.: Stanford University Press.

Glickman, C.D. (1985). *Supervision of Instruction: A Developmental Approach.* Boston: Allyn and Bacon.

Gould, S.J. (1981). *The Mismeasure of Man.* New York: W. W. Norton.

Guskey, T.R. (1986). "Staff Development and the Process of Teacher Change." *Educational Researcher* 15, 5: 5–12.

Holly, P., and G. Southworth. (1989). *The Developing School.* London: Falmer Press.

Kemmis, S., and R. McTaggart. (1988). *The Action Research Planner.* 3rd ed. Victoria, Australia: Deakin University Press.

Kidder, T. (1989). *Among Schoolchildren.* N.Y.: Houghton Mifflin.

"Learning from Children: Teachers Do Research." *Harvard Educational Letter* 4 (1988).

Lewin, K. (1947) "Frontiers in Group Dynamics." *Human Relations* 1.

Lewin, K. (1951). *Idem Field Theory in Social Science.* New York: Harper and Row.

Lieberman, A. (February 1986). "Collaborative Research: Work With, Not Working On." *Educational Leadership* 43, 5: 28–32.

Little, J.W. (Fall 1982). "Norms of Collegiality and Experimentation: Workplace Conditions of School Success." *American Educational Research Journal* 19, 3: 325–340.

Livingston, C., and S. Castle. (1989). *Teachers and Research in Action.* Washington, D.C.: National Education Association.

Mohr, M.M., and M.S. MacLean. (1987). *Working Together: A Guide for Teacher-Researchers.* Urbana, Ill.: National Council of

Teachers of English.

Olson, M.W., ed. (1990). *Opening the Door to Classroom Research.* Newark, Del.: International Reading Association.

Peabody Journal of Education. (Spring 1987). Theme Issue.

Puget Sound Educational Consortium. *Teacher Leadership.* Volumes 1, 3, 4, 5. Seattle: University of Washington.

Sagor, R. (December 1981). " 'A Day in the Life'—A Technique for Assessing School Climate and Effectiveness." *Educational Leadership* 39, 3: 190–193.

Sagor, R.D. (March 1991). "Collaborative Action Research: A Report from Project LEARN." *Educational Leadership* 48, 6: 6–10.

Saphier, J., and M. King. (March 1985). "Good Seeds Grow in Strong Cultures." *Educational Leadership* 42, 6: 67–74.

Schaefer, R. (1967). *The School as the Center of Inquiry.* New York: Harper and Row.

Schoen, D. (1983). *The Reflective Practitioner.* New York: Basic Books.

Schoen, D. (1987). *Educating the Reflective Practitioner: Toward a New Design for Teaching and Learning in the Professions.* San Francisco: Jossey-Bass Publishers.

Shulman, L.S. (1989). "Teaching Alone, Learning Together: Needed Agendas for the New Reforms." In *Schooling for Tomorrow: Directing Reforms to Issues that Count,* edited by T. Sergiovanni and J. Moore. Boston: Allyn and Bacon.

Tikunoff, W.J., and B.A. Ward. (March 1983). "Collaborative Research on Teaching." *The Elementary School Journal* 83, 1: 453–468.

Walker, R. (1985). *Doing Research: A Handbook for Teachers.* London: Methuen.

Wallace, M. (1987). "A Historical Review of Action Research: Some Implications for the Education of Teachers in Their Managerial Role." *Journal of Education for Teaching* 13, 2: 97–115.

About the Author

Richard Sagor left his position as a Professor of Education at Washington State University in August 1997 to found the Institute for the Study of Inquiry in Education, an organization committed to assisting schools and educators with their local school improvement initiatives.

During the past decade he has facilitated workshops on the conduct of collaborative action research throughout the United States and internationally. Sagor has 17 years of experience in public schools, including work as a teacher, principal, and assistant superintendent. He is a frequent contributor to *Educational Leadership* and the author of the ASCD book *Guiding School Improvement with Action Research.* His other books include *At-Risk Students: Reaching and Teaching Them, The TQE Principal: A Transformed Leader,* and *Local Control and Accountability: How to Get It, Keep It, and Improve School Performance.*

He can be reached at the Institute for the Study of Inquiry in Education (ISIE), Suite 103-239, 16420 SE McGillivray, Vancouver, WA 98683. Phone: 360-834-3503. E-mail: rdsagor@isie.org.